Standing through the Tears

I pray that you are encouraged & inspired.

Jawana Taylor 2012

Standing through the Tears

Tawana Taylor

Published by Tate Publishing & Enterprises, LLC
127 E. Trade Center Terrace | Mustang, Oklahoma 73064 USA
1.888.361.9473 | www.tatepublishing.com

Tate Publishing is committed to excellence in the publishing industry. The company reflects the philosophy established by the founders, based on Psalm 68:11,
"The Lord gave the word and great was the company of those who published it."

Cover design by Rodrigo Adolfo
Interior design by Mary Jean Archival

Published in the United States of America

ISBN: 978-1-62147-881-2
1. Poetry / Women Authors
2. Poetry / Subjects & Themes / Inspirational & Religious
12.09.19

Contents

A New Life

Your words have haunted me all my life, and now I've found a way of exposing you for who you were. You were bitter and cruel, hostile and mean. Your words went deep in my heart. They cut like a knife. I will never forget the nights I cried myself to sleep, listening to your taunts. I thought this would be the story of my life, the girl who would be nothing, the girl who would never measure up to anyone else in this world. You did all that you could to crush me and kill my spirit, but God had a different plan for my life. I would not die but live; I would not crumble and fall but rise from the ashes.

I now have a new story to tell, and this story has a new beginning. It begins with me standing on my feet, letting go of the shame and embarrassment of who I used to be.

I am no longer that little girl who would be nothing and who no one wanted to hear about.

My Story

No one knows my story
No one knows the tears I've cried
No one knows the darkness that surrounds me
No one knows the battles I fight

No one knows my story
No one knows the sacrifices I've made
No one knows the dreams I hold inside
No one knows the visions I dare to see

No one knows my story
No one knows the depth of despair I feel
No one knows the longings of my heart
No one knows the frustration I feel

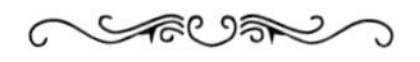

No one knows my story
No one knows my journey
No one knows my destiny
No one knows my testimony

Looking Back

I look in the mirror, and who do I see? I see a little girl full of hurt and pain. I see a little girl searching for love in all the wrong places. I see a little girl full of despair and longing. I see a little girl full of desperation. I see a little girl who has never known her worth.

I look in the mirror, and who do I see? I see a young lady filled with confusion. I see a young lady still searching for love. I see a young lady full of anger and loneliness. I see a young lady trapped by her emotions. I see a young lady who has never known her worth.

I look in the mirror, and who do I see? I see a young woman struggling through life. I see a young woman torn down from life's disappointments. I see a young woman trapped in her past. I see a young woman on the edge of disaster. I see a young woman searching for answers. I see a young woman who has never known her worth.

I look in the mirror, and who do I see? I see a mother, broken and confused. I see a mother ignoring the truth. I see a mother weeping herself to sleep at night. I see a mother gripping to maintain her life. I see a mother desperate and alone. I see a mother; she doesn't know where to turn. I see a mother searching for hope and love. I see a mother who has never known her worth.

I look in the mirror, and who do I see? I see a woman who has a lot to offer this world. I see a woman healed from life's bumps and bruises. I see a woman full of love and peace. I see a woman who knows her worth. I see a woman who won't ever look back. I see a woman who knows love and peace.

I look in the mirror, and who do I see?

I see myself.

I Cried

I cried when you rejected me. I cried when you humiliated me. I cried when you turned away from me. I cried when you looked at me with contempt in your eyes. I cried when you said you loved me no more. I cried when you looked at her with love and desire in your eyes. I cried when you walked away and never even said good-bye. I cried each time you chose them over me. I cried each time I thought of starting over. I cried each time you never looked my way. I cried myself to sleep each night. I cried for the emptiness and the void that loving you left in my heart. I cried for all the lies and betrayal that you chose to share with me. I cried for all the times I gave my body to you and you threw it away. I cried for the pieces of me that I will never get back. I cried for all the time that was lost while I loved you. I cried.

Good Morning, Heartache

Good morning, heartache; here we are again, facing another day
Good morning, heartache; how long will you stay
Good morning, heartache; when will I be free
Good morning, heartache; it's just you and me

Good morning, heartache; I cried myself to sleep
Good morning, heartache; I can't let anyone see
Good morning, heartache; please just let me be
Good morning, heartache; it's just you and me

Good morning, heartache; the sun seems so far away
Good morning, heartache; what will people say
Good morning, heartache; it was the month of May
Good morning, heartache; I must face another day

Good morning, heartache; here we are again
Good morning, heartache; you will not steal my heart again
Good morning, heartache; it's time to say good-bye
Good morning, heartache; never return again

Tired

Don't take me for granted. Don't take me for a fool. Don't think that I don't know any better because I do. Today, you showed me just how much you really love me. I now know that your love for me means nothing. I feel as though I've been abandoned, and there are lines that have to be drawn. This is where I draw the line. I'm tired of the excuses, I'm tired of the lies, and I'm tired of being taken for granted. I'm tired. I'm tired of feeling inferior to you, I'm tired of being frustrated, and I'm tired of loving you and you not loving me. I'm tired of being disappointed and heartbroken. I'm tired of crying and hiding my tears for fear of your disapproval. I'm tired of giving in to your wants while my needs go unmet. Don't take me for granted. Don't take me for a fool. Don't think that I don't know any better because I do. No longer will I allow you to walk over my feelings. I'm tired of being your doormat. I'm tired of waiting here, hoping you'll come home. I'm tired of sitting in the dark all alone. I'm tired of living in the shadows while life passes me by. I'm tired of being betrayed and having to suck it up. I'm tired. I'm tired. God help me, I'm tired.

What About Us?

I remember a time when talking and keeping in touch was important to us. I remember a time when spending time was important to us. I remember a time when we were important to us. What about us?

I know that as a relationship progresses, priorities can get lost in the shuffle of everyday life. Why is this? Have we begun to take one another for granted? Have we begun to only think about ourselves and our individual needs? What about us? Have we come to a point in this relationship where we are no longer living together but only existing together?

How do we get back to us? Do we even want to get back to us? These are questions that deserve honest answers. We spent more time talking and putting forth more of an effort to know one another not so long ago. We would talk on the phone for hours about everyday life and its challenges. We would talk for hours about what we wanted from this relationship and how we wanted this relationship to be different for the both of us. We used to talk of our hopes and dreams and how life had knocked us down but we found the strength to get back up. We talked about how fortunate and blessed we were to have found one another. We spoke often of our new life together and how we would help each other grow and be stronger. What about us?

How do we pick up the pieces and move forward without leaving us behind? How do we find a way to bridge the gap that is growing between us? How do we avoid growing lonely when we're still together? How do we face life's challenges together instead of apart? How do we define our individuality without erasing us?

The answers to these questions begin with one response: time. Time is something that passes very quickly and waits on no one.

Time is very precious and not to be taken lightly. Time can either heal old wounds or deepen old wounds. Time is a gift from God and should be treated as such. Time should be appreciated in all that we do.

Spending time together helps to renew the relationship on a daily basis. Spending time keeps us in remembrance of why we're together. Spending time helps keep us in remembrance of why we have chosen one another. Spending time helps us better understand what we need and have to offer one another. Spending time shows just how important the relationship is to both of us. Spending time keeps us connected so that we don't grow apart. Spending time can resolve minor issues before they become major problems. Spending time keeps the focus on the big picture and not just the narrow view. Spending time strengthens the relationship. Spending time can help to bridge the gap of individual weaknesses and turn them into united strengths. A lot can happen in one day, both individually and together.

Life offers many temptations and ways to avoid the truth, but quality time can help to conquer whatever life brings our way. Time is the most neglected part of a relationship because it's so easy to ignore. Spending time is more than just sharing the same space at the same time; it's reconnecting a bond that has somehow been broken. Spending time is hearing what you don't want to hear and saying what you might not want to say. But again, with time, this too becomes easier to do. I suppose the gist of the story is take time, make time, spend time.

What about us?

When Do I Celebrate?

When do I expect happiness?
When do I jump for joy?
When do I celebrate?

When do I stop searching for what I've never had?
When do I stop longing for what I've never known?
When do I celebrate?

When do I believe what you say?
When do I believe in you again?
When do I celebrate?

When do I let go of the fear?
When do I let the walls down?
When do I celebrate?

When do I feel like a treasure?
When do I feel loved without measure?
When do I celebrate?

When do I stop feeling like your burden?
When do I stop being your obligation?
When do I celebrate?

When do I celebrate?

Thinking of You

Hello, my dear. I was thinking of you and thought I'd drop you a line or two. I wanted to give you a few scriptures of encouragement, scriptures that have really helped me this past year.

I would like to start by saying I think you're a wonderful person with a kind heart, and I know that God has many good things in store for you. This is just the beginning of a beautiful journey for you and God. He has brought you to this point in your life for a reason, and He will manifest your purpose to you in due time. "To everything there is a season, and a time to every purpose under the heaven" (Ecclesiastes 3:1, KJV).

Everything that we experience is for our own good. Nothing that you've gone thru is in vain. "And we know that all things work together for good to them that love God, to them who are called according to his purpose" (Romans 8:28, KJV). When I reflect on these scriptures, I think of you and the wonderful destiny that's before you.

There is one other scripture I'd like to give to you.

> Trust in the Lord, and do good; so shalt thou dwell in the land, and verily thou shalt be fed. Delight thyself also in the Lord; and he shall give thee the desires of thine heart. Commit thy way unto the Lord; trust also in him; and he shall bring it to pass. And he shall bring forth thy righteousness as the light, and thy judgment as the noonday. Rest in the Lord, and wait patiently for him: fret not thyself because of him who prospereth in his way, because of the man who bringeth wicked devices to pass. Cease from anger, and forsake wrath: fret not thyself in any wise to do evil.
>
> Psalm 37:3-8 (KJV)

This particular book of psalms has kept me going when things have gotten to me or my mind was too occupied. I want you to know that God has a special place for you in His kingdom.

For Better or Worse

These are words that I ponder upon daily
I think about them when I awake and when I lay down
I think about these words as I think about my marriage

These are words that have come to haunt me
I think about them every time I lay alone at night
I think about these words as I look at my children

These are words that I choose to live by
I think about them each time I want to give up
I think about these words as I find the strength to continue on

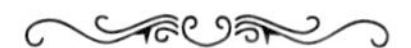

These are words not to be taken lightly
I think about them whenever I want to walk away
I think about these words each time I say, "Just one more day"

These are words that were spoken in love
I think about them each time my love grows cold
I think about these words as I learn the true meaning of love

These words were spoken as a commitment to God
I think about them whenever I seek a way out
I think about these words as I realize my word is my bond

Brother

I see you lying there, eyes shut, body so rigid. You're breathing but already lifeless. At first, I can't comprehend what is really happening. It doesn't seem real. I'm patiently waiting for you to wake up and say that everything is okay. You'll tell a joke, and we laugh. I can hear your voice so clearly, as if you're whispering in my ear. I can see you walking down Mama's hallway, entering the living room. You sit in her green chair and begin pestering me about nothing.

The children go crazy to see you. They give their love so freely and completely. Their eyes light up as if it were Christmas. My son wants to go back home with you, and you just got there. They saw a part of you that I never allowed myself to see. Oh, how I now long for that kind of emotional freedom, the innocence of a child's love. They don't have to see the failures, only the hopes of surprises to come. They love you completely and honestly.

I thank God that you were able to know the children and love them as you did. For that, I'll be forever grateful. When I look at them, I see you and me. Oh, what times we had, good and bad. Now, all I want to know are the good times and live them again. I love you and will never forget you.

Images in My Mind

Images of my brother lying in the hospital bed, stiff and motionless, haunt my mind today. I remember when we were kids playing outside in the summer, my brother trying to teach me how to play baseball, but I was too afraid of the ball.

Images of my dad lying in the hospital bed, a portrait of what used to be. I remember being a little girl full of excitement and anticipation to see him again.

I remember being a young woman seeking his advice about life. Oh, how I long for those days again.

Images of my brother and father continue to play in my mind, how similar they were and didn't even realize. They were both full of pain and rejection, but neither could admit it. They struggled for acceptance and love, both always being torn between the two.

Images of these two men will live with me forever, memories of pain and sorrow, memories of two lives that ended too soon. The funny thing about loss is that it stays with you in one form or another. Loss is an empty emotion that is never quite fulfilled. It's there just waiting to resurface again. People say that time heals all wounds, but this is not always true. Yes, time does make the pain of loss easier to deal with and less intense, but it's never quite forgotten.

Images of people past that haunt my mind. When will they end? I often ask myself this question, and I have yet to come up with an answer. What I do know is this. I must continue to live and press forward in spite of the pain and sorrow. I must rise to the challenge of seeking the peace of God in spite of these images. I know that in Him, I will find the answers to questions that linger in my mind. I know that with God, all things are possible, and this is what I must live by. I must remember that in life and death, God has a purpose and a season for all things.

My Brother

My brother, my friend, I'm sorry I didn't know how to love you. I wish I'd been a better sister, a more loving sister. Now that you're gone, there's a void that I can't explain. There's a place in my heart for only you. I never knew how deep my love was for you, how much we actually had in common. At the time, all I could see was our differences. Now all I can see is your pain, the pain that I wish I could take away, the loneliness that I so desperately want to replace with love. I've loved you all this time and never expressed it. I've felt your sorrows and hurts, and my heart breaks for you. Oh, how I wish I could somehow give you another life, a life very different than the one you knew, a life full of a father's love, the love that you so desperately needed and searched for in all the wrong people, the acceptance of a father's touch, a father's smile and approval, the unconditional love of the man that you were so much like. I love you. I love you, my brother, my friend.

MaDear

I hear you laughing about nothing.
I hear you call my name, requesting my presence.
I see you sitting there on your bed.
I see you hanging your head down, with arms crossed.

I enter the room; your hands are folded in your lap.
You begin to tell me a story.
The story you tell is one about life, your life.
I listen intently, waiting for another glimpse.
The glimpse will tell me more about you,
Who you are and where you come from,
Not just physically but mentally.

I find out more about who I am through your stories.
They tell me where I come from, the places
I've been and the places I dare to go.
Your stories tell of a time that will never be again, a
time that would be lost if not for your memories.

I see you sitting there on your bed, awaiting my response.
I see you hanging your head down, with arms crossed.
We look at one another, and it's as if we've
went back in time together.
I know who you are and where you've been.

Missing You

I thought I was over it, but I'm not
I pick up the phone to call, but I can't
I sometimes wonder what you're doing today
I still remember what used to be but is no more
I miss you so much, but I'm afraid to say it out loud
There's an empty place in my heart, but I don't know what to do
My life will never be the same without you, but I must go on

One day, I will remember you the way
you were, but today, I can't
One day, this will be my reality, but today, it's not
One day, my heart won't ache, but today, it does
One day, I'll be able to face my fears, but today, I can't
One day, I'll be able to speak of you out loud, but today, I won't
One day, this life will soon be over, but today, it's not
One day, I'll mourn no more, but I must go on

Baby Girl

Baby Girl, hold tight to your dreams
Life is not always what it seems.
You push and pull, rise and fall
A new day is coming; tear down the wall.

Baby Girl, live for today because tomorrow is not promised
In the pain of your yesterday lies the hope of today.
You stumble and struggle, rise and fall
A new day is coming; tear down the wall.

Baby Girl, hold tight to your dreams; take a look around
And then you'll see what God has given you to surround.
You moan and groan, rise and fall
A new day is coming; tear down the wall.

Baby Girl, hold tight to your dreams;
a promise is waiting for you to claim
There will be everlasting peace and unconditional
love; nothing will ever be the same.
You crawl and walk, rise and fall
A new day is coming; tear down the wall.

On the other side of the wall are love, peace, and understanding that only God can give. He'll wipe away the tears. He wants you to come back home. He wants you to know that His love is never far away. God will heal your pain and wipe away your tears. Be lonely no more; know that God is your everything and more. He'll hold you and comfort you in the middle of the night; He'll let you know that everything is all right. Tear down the wall, and you will see His outstretched arms waiting to carry you as far as you're willing to go. So, Baby Girl, hold tight to your dreams. This life is not what it seems. You'll rise and fall, so tear down the wall!

I Almost Let Go

I almost let go
But you heard my cry
I almost let go
But you dried my tears
I almost let go
But you didn't let me fall
I almost let go
But you placed my feet on solid ground
I almost let go
But you gave me strength
I almost let go
But you took away my fears
I almost let go
But you led the way
I almost let go
But you held my hand
I almost let go
But you set a new path
I almost let go...

I'm Here

I call your name, but you don't hear me.
I wipe away your tears, but you don't see me.
I reach out my hand, but you don't need me.
I lift up your heart, but you don't feel me.

I give to you all that I am, and yet you have no need for me.
I have given the ultimate sacrifice: my life.
What more would you ask of me?
I lift you up to my Father day and night.
I have left behind comfort, grace, and mercy until my return.
Comfort wiped your tears away.
Grace picked you up when you fell.
Mercy healed your heart and called you back home again.

I've called your name; will you answer?
I've wiped away your tears; will you see me?
I've lifted you back up on your feet; will you hold on?
I've taken away your hurt; will you let it go?

I'm right here waiting; all you have to do is call.
I'll never leave you nor forsake you.
I'll take care of all your needs.

You Loved Me

You loved me in spite of my shortcomings
You loved me even when I didn't love myself
You loved me in spite of rejection
You loved me even when I lost my way
You loved me in spite of disobedience
You loved me even when I went my own way
You loved me in spite of separation
You loved me even when I said no.

You loved me in spite of fear
You loved me even when I ran away
You loved me in spite of disappointment
You loved me even when I chose not to hear
You loved me in spite of disbelief
You loved me even when I lost faith
You loved me in spite of delay
You loved me even when I turned away

You loved me in spite of not trusting you
You loved me even when I took the wrong road
You loved me in spite of time
You loved me even when I came back home!

Look Around

I look around me, and I no longer like what I see.
The mood is so different now. Where's the trust?
You smile in my face and laugh behind my back.
Did you think I would not know?
Did you think things would ever be the same?

You look down from where you are as if you're better than I am.
You think that I don't know how things
really are, but this too shall pass.
One day soon, the truth will be exposed for
what it is and everyone will know.
Life is a journey that we all must travel, and in
our travels, we begin to discover who we are.
Life is full of hills and valleys, rivers
and streams, friends and foes.

At the end of the day, it's about how you travel through life's journeys.
Did you travel with care and compassion, or
did you travel with sticks and stones?
Did you carry arrogance and contempt in your baggage,
or did you carry meekness and forgiveness?
I don't know about you, but in spite of those
around me, I choose to be who God created me
to be and travel with care and compassion.
I choose to pack my baggage wisely and
consider every item's worth and value.
I now look around me, and I like what I see.
My trust is in the Lord, and things will never be the same again.

This Too Shall Pass

It's so true what they say. Misery does love company.

You can tell the people who are dissatisfied with themselves because they seem to seek out and find flaws within others.

These are the people who will never prosper in life and will wonder why not.

These are the people who will laugh on the outside while weeping on the inside.

They wear a mask to conceal who they really are; they want to be seen and heard while hiding behind the mask.

One day soon, this mask will come off and the true self will be made manifest.

There will be nothing to hide behind; no cynicism, no sarcasm, no alcohol to dull the pain.

There will only be truth and consequence. Yes, consequence for the blatant disregard for God's people. God will punish those who persecute His own.

Behind the scenes, you are very busy digging ditches and plotting mischief, but this too shall pass. "The wicked plotteth against the just, and gnasheth upon him with his teeth. The Lord shall laugh at him; for he seeth that his day is coming."

Your joy is only temporary and does not mean that you have succeeded in your attempts to belittle the righteous; you are a wolf in sheep's clothing, and soon, very soon, the world will know you for who you really are.

This Is Me

It's been almost a week to the day, and I still don't fully understand how I really feel. I do know that I still have some physical pain, but I can handle that. It's the mental, emotional part of me that I'm having the most difficulty sifting through and dealing with. I find myself alone and crying or in a room with someone else and yet still crying. I try to maintain as if everything is normal, as if the loss never happened, but the reality is that it did happen. For the first time in my life, I wanted something so bad I could believe in it, and now it's gone. This is the part of me that I can't share. This is the part of me that only I know about.

No, I have not forgotten the many blessings that God has given me, blessings that I surely did not deserve. I tell myself to get over it and move on. The past is the past, and there is nothing I can do about it now, but there's also this voice inside my head that says I could have done more. The voice tells me that this was somehow my fault. I try to pick up the pieces and I fall. I fall to the floor and cry out. God, please help me right now! God, please forgive me of my sins, please give me a second, third, and even a fourth chance to prove myself worthy of You. I will do better. Just heal me, oh Lord. Give me peace of mind and peace in my heart. God, please tell me all the plans that You've made for me. God, hold me near You and tell me that everything will be just fine. Tell me that I will be just fine. Please, God, reassure me that You have me in the palms of Your hands and You won't let me go. Tell me that no matter what, You love me, dear Lord.

I do not know what's going to happen next, what changes are before me, but I do know that I cannot do it without God. I know that God is the only one to know what waits before me. Only God knows my true purpose and the reason certain situations are allowed to happen in my life. The only truth I have to hold on to is my hope and my faith in God to get me through this test. I have to believe that in this test lies my testimony. Lord, I thank you for hearing my cry and delivering me from the depths of despair. Lord, I'm thanking You in advance for freeing my mind from self-doubt and turmoil. Lord, I thank You for giving me the victory.

My Life

I left the house not knowing where to go and having no one to turn to. I drove to the church, where I sat in my truck and cried and cried until there was nothing left. I tried reading a few scriptures, and then the tears started again. I didn't want to go back, but I had nowhere else I could go. I had no friends to call, no one to talk to. I felt alone and desperate. I felt as if I was at the end of my rope. I wanted to leave and never look back. I didn't want to be me anymore. I wanted no part of my life any more. I just wanted to be free—free from hurt and pain, free from disappointment, free from loneliness.

For a while now, I have been living in turmoil. I haven't been really happy in about a year, not with myself and not with my life. It's been one something after another. I go through each day as if everything is fine; I try to wear a smile on the outside because inside I am fighting to live. My flesh wants to die, but my spirit just wants to live. I have nothing significant left to give to those closest to me. I'm drained. I'm burned out. I feel as though I'm the only one fighting for my family. The enemy is attacking and trying to kill the most important thing to me, and I'm the only one putting up a fight. I can't do this on my own, but if I gave up, who would fight for me? Who would fight for my children and my husband? God, give me the strength I need to make it through these tests and trials.

My body is tired and weak, but I must continue on. I must run the race until the end. I'm out of breath and thirsty. My heart is beating so fast I think it might come out of my chest. I try to hold on with all my strength, but it's not enough. I hear myself cry out to God, "I've fallen and I can't get up." Save me, oh Lord, for You are the only one who can. If God doesn't save me, I won't be saved. I hear His voice in my sleep, telling me to wait. This is what I will do. I will wait on the Lord, for He is my rock and my salvation. Through my weakness, He shall be made strong. I might be down, but I'm not out. I might be weak, but I'm not giving up. God has been too good to me to give up now. I know that all of this is for a divine purpose that God has for me. One day soon, I will tell my story and give my testimony about how I made it through. I will tell others about how God picked me up and brought me out and that when I had no one else to lean on, God was my rock. When I had no one else around me to trust, I trusted God, and He was there every time. When I was at my lowest in life, God delivered me from the pits of hell.

As I sit here and write, I wait for God to finish the work that He has started in me. I wait for God to set me free. I wait for God to say, "Rejoice, my daughter, for you have done well."

I Am

I am adored by God; I am beautiful and blessed by His anointing
I am cared for and cherished by His heart; I am determined and driven by His faith in me
I am encouraged through His Word; I am favored with His presence
I am graced with His love; I am humbled by His awesome power
I am imprinted with His glory; I am joyed by His music
I am kept safe in His pavilion; I am loved by the King of kings
I am moved by his devotion, and I am never alone without a Comforter
I am overcome by His omnipotence; I am protected by His angels
I am quickened by His breath, and I am restored by His forgiveness
I am strengthened by His compassion; I am trusted with trials and tribulations
I am uniquely created with a purpose, and I am victorious in fighting His battles
I am a woman of God

No More Tears

I no longer cry when I think of you. I no longer cry when I see you with another woman. I no longer cry when I think of my wasted time. I no longer cry when I feel lonely. I no longer cry for you in the middle of the night. I no longer cry for the touch of your hand. I no longer cry for your absence. I no longer cry to have you back. I no longer cry when you look the other way. I no longer cry because I was never chosen first. I no longer cry for the lost pieces of my life. I no longer cry. I now know that in the humiliation was my victory. I no longer cry. I rejoice!

Every Woman

A battle rages inside me. I don't know what to do. I feel myself drowning, but can't keep my head above water. I'm so used to putting everyone else before me; I find that I don't have time for myself.

Throughout the course of any given day, I play many roles. I am a wife to my husband. I must assess what his needs are for the day and keep the lines of communication open between us. I must remember that I am not only his wife but I am also his friend, a shoulder to lean on in times of stress, a voice of wisdom in times of confusion, a listening ear in times of frustration, an encouraging word in times of insecurity.

I am a mother to my children, preparing them one day at a time for what life might throw their way. I must set an example of what I want their lives to be a reflection of. It is my responsibility to instill godly values and morals that will stay with them wherever they might go. I must show them how to survive in a world that takes no prisoners. I want them to know that whatever trials and tribulations they might face, I am only a prayer away. My love is forever unconditional.

I am a daughter to my parents with responsibilities to them for the sacrifices they made on my behalf. I always had food on the table; clothes on my back; and a nice, cozy bed to lay my head. My mother always made it look so easy, but being a mother myself, I now know that it wasn't as easy as she made it seem. There was great sacrifice on her part. No childhood is perfect, and as children, we can't fully appreciate the sacrifices of our parents. There is so much that they go without for the sake of our happiness and well-being. I remember the struggles placed upon her shoulders so that my brother and I had these essentials. I must now do my best to make sure my mother has to struggle no more. The words and advice that my father planted in my soul are irreplaceable. Nothing can take the place of wisdom from father to daughter, words of acceptance, advice, and affirmation. These are words that shaped my life and, in turn, caused me to think about the decisions I had to make in life.

I am also a woman at the end of the day with needs and wants that have been pushed aside. There just doesn't seem to be enough time in the day. I'm on the go form sunrise to sunset. Everyone needs a little piece of me, and at the end of the day, I find myself all given out. I must function with lack of sleep, lack of proper rest and diet. I find myself on the treadmill of life, so easy to slip right off. There are a few things I've come to realize, and that is, if I don't take care of me, I won't be around to take care of anyone else.

I must learn to start the day off with a proper breakfast that consists of seeking the Lord before I start my day. "I love them that love me, and those that seek me early shall find me" (Proverbs 8:17, KJV).

I must learn to make time for lunch daily, which consists of constant prayer. "Be careful for nothing; but in every thing by prayer and supplication with thanksgiving let your requests be made known unto God" (Philippians 4:6, KJV).

I must learn to eat dinner early in the evening to restore my strength. "But they that wait upon the Lord shall renew their strength; they shall mount up with wings as eagles; they shall run, and not be weary; and they shall walk and not faint" (Isaiah 40:31, KJV).

I must learn to give thanks to God before going to sleep at night. "In everything give thanks: for this is the will of God in Christ Jesus concerning you" (1 Thessalonians 5:18, KJV).

I must learn to rest in the Lord and trust Him completely. "Therefore my heart is glad, and my glory rejoiceth: my flesh also shall rest in hope" (Psalm 16:9, KJV).

As a woman, I must learn how to give to others as well as myself without going hungry. I have to consistently feed myself a proper diet and get the proper rest. If I follow these simple instructions, I can be restored and strengthened continually while taking care of those whom God has placed in my care.

[1] (Psalm 37:12, 13; KJV).